Story Craft II
A Born Storytellers Workbook

About the Born Storytellers

The Born Storytellers is a program of creative writing created by Kevin Price, teaching students the craft of story writing. It began in 2005 and has been a regular part of the curriculum in several Western Australian schools from junior primary classes through to upper high schools. Since its inception, the Born Storytellers has published more than 40 anthologies of students' work and edited and published over 500 young authors, many of whom have gone on to further literary studies.

More information can be found at www.bornstorytellers.net

Kevin Price

Kevin Price has been earning his living as a writer and creative consultant since 1988, starting as a magazine columnist and advertising copywriter. He developed an interest in story and the theories behind the craft of writing stories in the early 1990s and considers himself, apart from a writer of them, to be a long term student of story. He has been teaching the Born Storytellers program of story craft to Western Australian students, both children and adult learners in schools and writers centres since 2005. He is currently enrolled as a PhD candidate in English and Creative Writing at Murdoch University in Western Australia.

Story Craft II
A Born Storytellers Workbook

Kevin Price BA (English & Creative Arts)

CROTCHET QUAVER

Published in 2014 by Crotchet Quaver
119 Ridgewood Loop Bullsbrook Western Australia 6084

© Kevin Price 2014

This publication is copyright. Subject to statutory exceptions and provisions of fair dealing under the Copyright Act 1968, no part of this work may be reproduced without the written permission of the publishers. The moral rights of the author have been asserted.

Reproduction for educational purposes

The Australian Copyright Act 1968 allows a maximum of one chapter or 10% of the pages of this work, whichever is the greater, to be reproduced or communicated by any educational instutution for its educational purposes provided that the institution (or the body that administers it) has given a remuneration notice to Copyright Agency Limited (CAL).

A CIP catalogue record for this book is available from the National Library of Australia.

All inquiries should be addressed to the publisher.
Crotchet Quaver
119 Ridgewood Loop Bullsbrook Western Australia 6084

ISBN: (paperback) 978-0-9875402-8-7

Contents

A story planning process	6
Tackling your project	9
Step 1: Find and develop your ideas	11
Step 2: Create your main character	28
Step 3: Populate your story	47
Step 4: Create your story world	56
Step 5: Conflict	75
Step 6: Develop your plot and step sheet	81
Moving ahead	93

A Story Planning Process

Use the following outline to guide you through the story planning process. Once you have established a story idea you will need to push and pull it to shape it and make it set imaginations on fire. This process is not necessarily linear: revisit it as you work through your story development to help keep you on track. Make sure you keep a separate notebook of 'notes and thoughts' to house 'arrivals' as they appear.

Develop the story idea

1. Find unusual ideas in the news, in your family history or with an unusual artifact, and through observations of people and places around you. Develop an idea of what you want to write about, who is involved and what happens to them. Dream on it. Sketch brief and unconnected moments in your notebook.

2. Establish a premise for your story. The premise is: '*Character* through *conflict* leads to *conclusion*.' (Substitute Character, Conflict and Conclusion for the specific elements of your story.) This guides you in exploring what you want to write about.

3. Write a one or two sentence snapshot of the story. 'This story is about … (what someone did to get what they want)'.

Identify and create the principle characters

4. Develop the identities of the principal characters involved. (Write character sketches of at least the Protagonist and Antagonist.)

   - To profile them write

     a. A paragraph describing their Physicality

     b. A paragraph describing their Sociology

     c. A paragraph describing their Psychology

   - Be clear about their goals: what each of them wants; define their talents and weaknesses

- Describe the things that make them different from others; identify their hidden psychological needs

- Interview them to get an understanding of their ruling passions

- Write a journal entry from each main character's point of view

Map out the setting and oppositions

5. Map the relative archetypal positions and relationships of each character. Develop simple profiles of the minor characters; more complex profiles of the major characters.

6. Establish your story world; detail the locations and settings where your story will take place. Map out the settings so you know how the land lies, where you can build in obstacles and places your characters can call home. Identify the time of the story, detail the physical, social and technological elements; the natural and man-made aspects of the story world.

7. Describe the central conflict of the story — what is being fought over? Define the ways the main characters will oppose each other over the central conflict; examine how the story world plays into the conflict.

Create the structure and sequence of events

8. Consider the seven basic plots and define the basic form of your story. Try to determine a genre for the story. Consider how a different genre might change it.

9. Outline the story's sequences in a step sheet

   - Use a lined page and list the sequences (one thing leads to another), or

   - Write each sequence on a small card and lay them out in an order that works best — change the order around and see how it alters the story.

10. Know the ending of the story. Determine how it will end, what leads to the climax, and what follows it.

11. Test your story plan against our earlier definition of a story: does it have a series of consequential episodes, worthy human characters, and is there a moment of transformation?

An Outline Of The Program

Week 1	The story idea, premise & snapshot
Week 2	Creating characters
Week 3	Mapping a story world
Week 4	Understanding conflict & oppositions
Week 5	Defining a plot and mapping out structure
Week 6	Writing techniques for scenes, dialogue and POV
Week 7	
	Write your draft
Week 8	
Week 9	Editing practice

Tackling Your Project

This book is the practical part of the Born Storytellers Story Craft program. You need to refer to sections of Born Storytellers I which has been supplied to you in a separate format in order to develop a knowledge of the theories you are applying in this book. The following pages set out the project process outlined above. Each step represents one stage in the story planning process, beginning with techniques for finding and developing a story idea.

This is challenging work and requires substantial commitment to work progressively and systematically. The process of story creation and story writing is a combination of creative and critical thinking, of imaginative and logical processing.

You need to spend time on both aspects — on dreaming and thinking, and on writing and note taking. It is often a very difficult task to think of a story to write.

Work a little bit on this every day. Twenty minutes spent every day is two hours and twenty minutes a week. It is far more effective to spend twenty minutes a day every day, than it is to spend a concentrated two hours once a week. The reasons are simple: it's easier to find a regular twenty minutes than a single block of two hours, the story is with you every day — you don't have to start from scratch to remember where you were, and you will be amazed at how much you can achieve in smaller blocks of time.

I have deliberately included additional and alternate exercises in some steps. This is because some exercises are more accessible than others, they can be easier to complete, and because sometimes you may want to go a little further with your ideas. This is intended to be a flexible program, but at the end of the planning phase, you should have completed enough of the steps set out in the list above to be able to stand up and 'pitch' the story you are going to write as if you were pitching it to a publisher. In order to do that, you must 'know' your story.

Most importantly, I don't want you to feel overwhelmed by this process. However, there is a school of thought that 'writing stories is easy and it just comes to you.' This is not the case. The truth is that writing a great story is very difficult and you have to work at. All successful writers work at it every day. This project is to show you some of the things that you have to work at in order to be a writer. I don't expect that you will master all of these practices in the one project, or two. It is to give you an experience that I know will help you in all of your writing, both creative and critical.

Test your Knowledge

To answer the following questions, you need to have read the chapter: The Narrative, the Episodes and the Transformation from *Story Craft I*

QUIZ #1

What are the key concepts of a story?

Something ....

A Worthy .... wants something and acts to get it

A narrative of ....

Designed to ....

A premise is:

◯ A place to put your school bag

◯ A short statement that tells a moral

◯ An expression of character through conflict leads to conclusion

◯ A powerful god

Four important parts of a story idea:

What are the four key things that your story idea should have?

1 ....

2 ....

3 ....

4 ....

Step 1: Find and Develop Your Ideas

This step has three parts. First you need to find and develop a selection of ideas; then create a premise and a snapshot statement of the one you will turn into a story.

READINGS: THE NARRATIVE, THE EPISODES AND THE TRANSFORMATION (Story Craft I)

1 Finding ideas

Ideas are all around us: they're in the news, lying around the pages of books, hidden in family secrets and strange objects, occur when strangers meet . . . there is no shortage of ideas. This process requires a bit of time spent looking around you for ideas that show promise for intrigue, a unique twist, colourful character and an unusual item, object or moment. Exercises 1.1 - 1.3 are different ways you can uncover story ideas. Try to explore all three sources of ideas to generate at least a dozen ideas or more to choose from. Record what you discover on the following pages.

But before you do, answer the following quick quiz about yourself:

QUIZ #2

List three things that:

a) Worry you the most

----

b) Make you the most excited

----

c) If changed, would make the world a better place

EXERCISE 1.1 Search the News

Search some news articles on internet news sites, reading stories that affect you in some way, or in particular affect the issues you raised in Quiz #2, and make you think they have the potential for a story.

Write down the basic idea of the article as it is reported.

Some good news sites might include:

www.abc.net.au

www.bbc.co.uk

www.nytimes.com

www.aljazeera.com

. . . and many other traditional news sources.

But you might also look at magazine sites such as:

www.madmagazine.com

www.cracked.com

. . . and other satirical and humour magazines.

www.onlinenewspapers.com lists worldwide online newpapers and magazines.

A google search for the term 'weird headlines' returns about 22 million entries, listing many websites that feature 'odd and funny news headlines', 'latest bizarre news stories', 'strange-but-true stories', and many more. Many radio station sites also broadcast strange story happenings.

In addition to how the article might address the issues you listed in Quiz #2, consider the following aspects:

- Are the circumstances being described usual or unusual?
- Are the people involved normal people or unusual?
- Is the situation being addressed in a usual or unusual way?

EXAMPLE 1.1

>Four black swans captured on video surfing on a Queensland Gold Coast beach. (smh.com.au Dec 2013) After the local government at Kirra in Qld had spend 1.1 million dollars on returning the waves to the beach, four black swans - tourists in themselves - were captured on video surfing a succession of waves. Other beach goers were seen interacting with the swans in the shallows. (People in a usual setting meeting with unusual circumstances.)

>Woman Buried Alive, Funeral Goers Hear Screams From The Grave (dailybuzzlive.com Oct 2014) A Chicago funeral director tried to murder his 34 year old estranged wife by substituting her drugged body for the real corpse at a funeral. The woman was discovered by a family remaining at the graveside of their son's funeral service who heard screams coming from beneath ground. (Unusual circumstances with usual people.)

>Scary Clown Terrorizes British Town (livescience.com September 2013) Who is wearing the disguise of a clown seen in different parts of Northampton: is it a kindly grandfather or a serial killer? Is there a danger if others start copying the antics and more clowns appear, scaring people and using the clown disguise as a way of committing offences? (Unusual person in a usual situation.)

Write your news articles here...

EXERCISE 1.2 Research your Family

Most of our families have secrets and oddities involving people and events of the past. You can begin by searching through old family photographs or diaries and asking family members about the people, places, objects and technology depicted in them.

You may find members of your family have experienced an unusual place, a fright, an accident, an injury, a crime or injustice, a romance gone wrong (or accidently right), or a terrible break up. These are all good fodder for a story idea.

Is there an object, such as an heirloom, or old piece of technology that might trigger an unusual tale? Great family stories can be found by discussing grandparents who fought in wars, parents who lived through hard times, miracle cures, sudden fortunes, unfortunate deaths and the like.

Write out the 'thing' you would explore, again paying attention to your lists from Quiz #2 and the following:

- Are the circumstances being described usual or unusual?
- Are the people involved normal people or unusual?
- Is the situation being addressed in a usual or unusual way?

EXAMPLE 1.2

> In our family, we had sets of crockery as children that were painted with 'bunnykins' images. I once saw an old photograph that brought back memories of those plates. I then figured out how I could tell a story of loss and nature's brutality. See *The Lock House*.

Write your observations here…

EXERCISE 1.3 Observation

Writing always begins with an observation of some sort. Observation is the practice of seeing, hearing, smelling, tasting and touching the world around you.

Observation as a creative practice is difficult because you need to do it consciously and note down things you observe as you go about your day. Stories are about change, so it makes some sense to spend time observing change.

Sit and observe a place for just 15 minutes (you can do it longer, or repeat it) and jot down the changes you see from moment to moment: the shifts in light, temperature, wind, shadow; the comings and goings of people, animals, insects, traffic, aircraft, clouds … Note changes in the ground, dust and changing colours.

Write down your observations and try to identify an issue of *intrigue, a unique twist, a colourful character and/ or an unusual item, object or moment.*

Remember, you are looking for the following:

- Are the circumstances being described usual or unusual?
- Are the people involved normal people or unusual?
- Is the situation being addressed in a usual or unusual way?

EXAMPLE 1.3

> This was a five minute observation on my verandah (7/11/2014) …
>
> *Green, unripened tomatoes are scattered on the ground, removed from the vine and dropped two metres away. By what? Teeth marks and gouging puncture the skin, some of the interior of the fruit eaten, gnawed … the clouds blot the sun and the colours no longer shine, a gentle breeze pushes the lemon grass leaves in lazy swats, as overhead the crickets and cicadas snap their rhythm like a tambourine player, the roof creaking as the sun goes off the boil and a parrot in the distance squawking like door on rusty hinges opening and closing. A dog barks in the distant left as a plane groans its way into the air, its murmur eventually cloaked by a swift breeze that whooshes through the leaves and pushes the clouds out of the sun's path.*
>
> Note that this piece is not edited, it has a lack of sentence breaks and moves from one observation to another as changes occur and as phenomena come to my notice. I doubt that the crickets and cicadas suddenly started up, more that I hadn't noticed them earlier. This is how observation works. You must make yourself available to the sensations around you. Simply write what you observe as it occurs, write quickly without judgement or editing.

2. Developing Ideas

Not every initial idea is going to pan out — many times ideas just don't seem to go anywhere. It doesn't matter. The more you do, the more you will become aware of ideas that have potential. And not only that, you never know when one idea you captured today will be useful while you are working on your story; when you are stuck, all you have to do is trawl through your idea bank for fresh inspiration.

This is when you get creative.

Take each idea and ask 'What if …' of the idea, always looking for the answer to be what someone did to get what they wanted. Then add the question, 'and …' to extend the idea a little further. Be creative, be daring, be ridiculous! Yes, ridiculous! Test the ideas with absolutely absurd propositions. You can explore each idea with several *What if?… and …* scenarios. You can combine one or more, or splice one into parts. Try to work quickly, challenge yourself to stretch your imagination beyond the ordinary and mundane. Try changing the genders of the people involved, try shifting the ideas into different genres, try going back in time, going forwards in time … there are many ways you can explore each idea.

EXAMPLE 2.1

> What if the swans are really robots from a technology company and they are stealing data from mobile phones used to photograph them …
>
> What if the animal taking the tomatoes was the Northampton Clown and he could move through time and space, controlling light and wind …?

Try to expand at least three different ideas with 'What it … and …?'

3. Refining your Idea

From the first two parts of this exercise, you should have somewhere around a dozen workable ideas. From your list, *choose 3* that appeal to you because they have the potential to fulfil what you want to write about. For each idea:

IDEA 1

What is intriguing about the idea?

What unique twist could happen in the end?

Who is the colourful character?

What unusual item, object or moment is involved?

IDEA 2

What is intriguing about the idea?

What unique twist could happen in the end?

Who is the colourful character?

What unusual item, object or moment is involved?

IDEA 3

What is intriguing about the idea?

What unique twist could happen in the end?

Who is the colourful character?

What unusual item, object or moment is involved?

---

4. Writing a snapshot story statement

With the story idea(s) you feel strongest about, try to summarise the story idea as a story snapshot statement: *Replace the sections in brackets with the specifics of your idea.*

This story is about [*someone*] who [*had something happen*] and then [*did something*] to [*get what they wanted*]

Eg: The Lock House. This story is about a man who saw a red jumper and recalled a tragedy to reflect on a loss.

5. Creating a premise

Take the story idea and decide what is important about the idea that you want to write about.

What does it mean to you personally?

Eg: The Lock House. The memory triggered by an observation.

What point would you like to make?

Eg: The Lock House. Nostalgia can be a painful experience.

How does the character end up?

Eg: The Lock House. Melancholy. Reminded of an event long ago.

What human condition does the character go through?

Eg: The Lock House. Helplessness in the face of the power of nature.

Your premise: [*character through conflict leads to conclusion*]

Eg: Memory leads to pain.

Step 2: Create Your Main Characters

This exercise involves a good deal of creative energy and writing. You need to get to know the main character in your story. And then you need to repeat the process to get to know your main character's nemesis.

READINGS: THE REIGN OF HOMO FICTUS (Story Craft I)

1 Your Protagonist

The Process

Study the list of character attributes in the following table and work through it, listing some of the details of your character in the space on the next page. (Complete as many of the following details as you can but address at least three details in each column. Remember, any decisions you make now can always be changed later.) You may also find you need to return to this list from time to time.

PHYSICAL	SOCIOLOGICAL	PSYCHOLOGICAL
Gender	Social class: Lower, Middle, Upper, Working, Monied, Management, Creative	Sexuality: Orientation, Engagement, Moral values
Age	Occupation (work or school): Type of work, Hours of work, Income, Conditions of work, Attitude towards work, Suitability for work…	Personal ambition and desire
Ethnicity	Education: Level, Kinds of schools, Marks, Relationships with teachers/other students	Frustrations and chief disappointments
Height and weight	Home life: Family structure, Parentage, Character's Marital status	Temperament: Angry, Easygoing, Joyful, Pessimist, Optimist
Colours: Hair, Eyes, Skin, Clothing…	Religion	Attitude towards life: Resigned, Militant, Defeatist
Posture: Walking style, Bearing	Race, Nationality	Complexes: Obsessions, Inhibitions, Superstitions, Phobias
Appearance: Attractiveness, Over/under weight, Cleanliness, Neatness	Place in community	Personality: Extrovert, Introvert, Ambivert, Intuitive, Judging, Idealist, Artist, Rationalist
Shapes: Head, Face, Ears, Limbs	Political affiliations	Abilities: Languages, Talents, Skills
Health	Amusement and leisure	Qualities: Imagination, Judgement, Taste, Poise
Defects: Deformities … Abnormalities … Birthmarks … Diseases (history as well as any current) …		IQ level
Language and speaking style …		Happiness

Character Attributes

List some of details that help identify your character.

Character Name ....

PHYSICAL	SOCIOLOGICAL	PSYCHOLOGICAL

Commentary and a Short Biography of Your Protagonist

Sometimes it helps to draw a picture of your character. (There is a blank page you can use on page 33.) However, if you draw your character, be sure to make notes on the drawing about specific details, such as colours (eyes, hair, skin), clothes (colours, shapes, styles), attitude (how the character stands and speaks) and so on …

From the details you have listed on the previous page, write a short, structured biography of the character, covering the major stages of his/her life and the significant events that have caused changes. This biography should try to explore relationships with the character's parents, and others they grew up with that helped shape the character. In particular, you should try to map out the biography through the story, from before the story begins to after it finishes. Try to paint an interesting picture of the character. You can write the biography in either first or third-person point of view.

Write your biography here (300 –500 words)

Illustrate your character here…

Interview your Protagonist

On paper, conduct an interview of your character, from *one* of the following perspectives. Either:

1. *Arrest report*. Imagine you are a detective investigating a crime that may or may not have anything to do with your character directly. Find out about your character's relationships, make judgements about his honesty and infallibility, try to establish the detective's impression of a character type, establish the character's recent history, attitude towards the crime. Your character might be hiding her drug habit while the police are investigating the murder of her next door neighbour. Be thorough.

2. *A job interview*. You are interested in hiring the character for a job. Find out about the character's work history and achievements, her attitudes towards social responsibility as it might apply to your workplace, her qualifications, marital status, ability to work beyond hours … be pretty demanding here. Remember, if you give her the job, you expect her to deliver, but you might also discover something darker and more interesting. Note: Expect your character to lie.

3. *A celebrity interview*. Your character has achieved something that is newsworthy and you are the journalist charged with interviewing her and reporting on the situation. As a journalist, you expect certain things from your interviewees — it may be easy or hard to get what you want. Be on guard for demurral and obfuscation — remember characters lie, cheat, demur, cloud the facts … yours could be doing all of them and more.

Write you interview here…

2 Your Antagonist

Developing your Antagonist is as important as developing your Protagonist — a story is only as good as the contest between the Protagonist and the Antagonist. Your Antagonist must be more than an equal to your Protganonist. Work through exactly the same process for your Antagonist as you did for your Protagnist.

The Process

Study the list of character attributes in the following table and work through it, listing some of the details of your character. (Complete as many of the following details as you can. Remember, any decisions you make now can always be changed later.) You may also find you need to return to this list from time to time.

PHYSICAL	SOCIOLOGICAL	PSYCHOLOGICAL
Gender	Social class: Lower, Middle, Upper, Working, Monied, Management, Creative	Sexuality: Orientation, Engagement, Moral values
Age	Occupation (work or school): Type of work, Hours of work, Income, Conditions of work, Attitude towards work, Suitability for work…	Personal ambition and desire
Ethnicity	Education: Level, Kinds of schools, Marks, Relationships with teachers/other students	Frustrations and chief disappointments
Height and weight	Home life: Family structure, Parentage, Character's Marital status	Temperament: Angry, Easygoing, Joyful, Pessimist, Optimist
Colours: Hair, Eyes, Skin, Clothing…	Religion	Attitude towards life: Resigned, Militant, Defeatist
Posture: Walking style, Bearing	Race, Nationality	Complexes: Obsessions, Inhibitions, Superstitions, Phobias
Appearance: Attractiveness, Over/under weight, Cleanliness, Neatness	Place in community	Personality: Extrovert, Introvert, Ambivert, Intuitive, Judging, Idealist, Artist, Rationalist
Shapes: Head, Face, Ears, Limbs	Political affiliations	Abilities: Languages, Talents, Skills
Health	Amusement and leisure	Qualities: Imagination, Judgement, Taste, Poise
Defects: Deformities … Abnormalities … Birthmarks … Diseases (history as well as any current) …		IQ level
Language and speaking style …		Happiness

Character Attributes

List some of details that help identify your character.

Character Name ....

PHYSICAL	SOCIOLOGICAL	PSYCHOLOGICAL

Commentary and a Short Biography of Your Antagonist

Sometimes it helps to draw a picture of your character. (There is a blank page you can use on page 42.) However, if you draw your character, be sure to make notes on the drawing about specific details, such as colours (eyes, hair, skin), clothes (colours, shapes, styles), attitude (how the character stands and speaks) and so on …

From the details you have listed, write a short, structured biography of the character, covering the major stages of his/her life and the significant events that have caused changes. This biography should try to explore relationships with the character's parents, and others they grew up with that helped shape the character. In particular, you should try to map out the biography through the story, from before the story begins to after it finishes. Try to paint an interesting picture of the character. You can write the biography in either first or third-person point of view.

Write your biography here (300 –500 words)

Illustrate your character here...

Interview your Antagonist

On paper, conduct an interview of your character, from *one* of the following perspectives. Either:

1. *Arrest report*. Imagine you are a detective investigating a crime that may or may not have anything to do with your character directly. Find out about your character's relationships, make judgements about his honesty and infallibility, try to establish the detective's impression of a character type, establish the character's recent history, attitude towards the crime. Your character might be hiding her drug habit while the police are investigating the murder of her next door neighbour. Be thorough.

2. *A job interview*. You are interested in hiring the character for a job. Find out about the character's work history and achievements, her attitudes towards social responsibility as it might apply to your workplace, her qualifications, marital status, ability to work beyond hours … be pretty demanding here. Remember, if you give her the job, you expect her to deliver, but you might also discover something darker and more interesting.

3. *A celebrity interview*. Your character has achieved something that is newsworthy and you are the journalist charged with interviewing her and reporting on the situation. As a journalist, you expect certain things from your interviewees — it may be easy or hard to get what you want. Be on guard for demurral and obfuscation — remember characters lie, cheat, demur, cloud the facts … yours could be doing all of them and more.

Write you interview here…

3 Discuss the differences

Review your biography of the Protagonist against the one of the Antagonist and make a list of the key differences, particularly those that will cause conflict, or make the conflict more intense.

Step 3: Populate Your Story

READINGS: WHO ELSE IS IN THE PLAYGROUND? (Story Craft I)

EXERCISE 3.1 List Others Involved

Draw up a list of the characters most directly related to your main character in your story and briefly describe their relationship with the main character and with each other. Try to identify the circumstances that connect them. Be creative about who is involved and why. Keep in mind all the while what the Protagonist wants — what the Antagonist wants to prevent the Protagonist from obtaining. One useful way of doing this is to draw a type of 'mind map'. Put your Protagonist in the centre and connect other characters, explaining their roles by what they do, and the relationship they have with the Protagonist. Draw a diagram. Use lots of notations.

List your characters here...

EXERCISE 3.2 Map Out Your Core Archetypes

From your list of other characters (above), use the following to identify your characters and place them in their relevant archetypal positions and discuss the ways in which they interact with the Protagonist. Use the following exercise to analyse your characters' relationships with your Protagonist and among themselves. Identify those who act within the realms of the core archetypes and discuss the kinds of influences they might have on the main character's progress through the story.

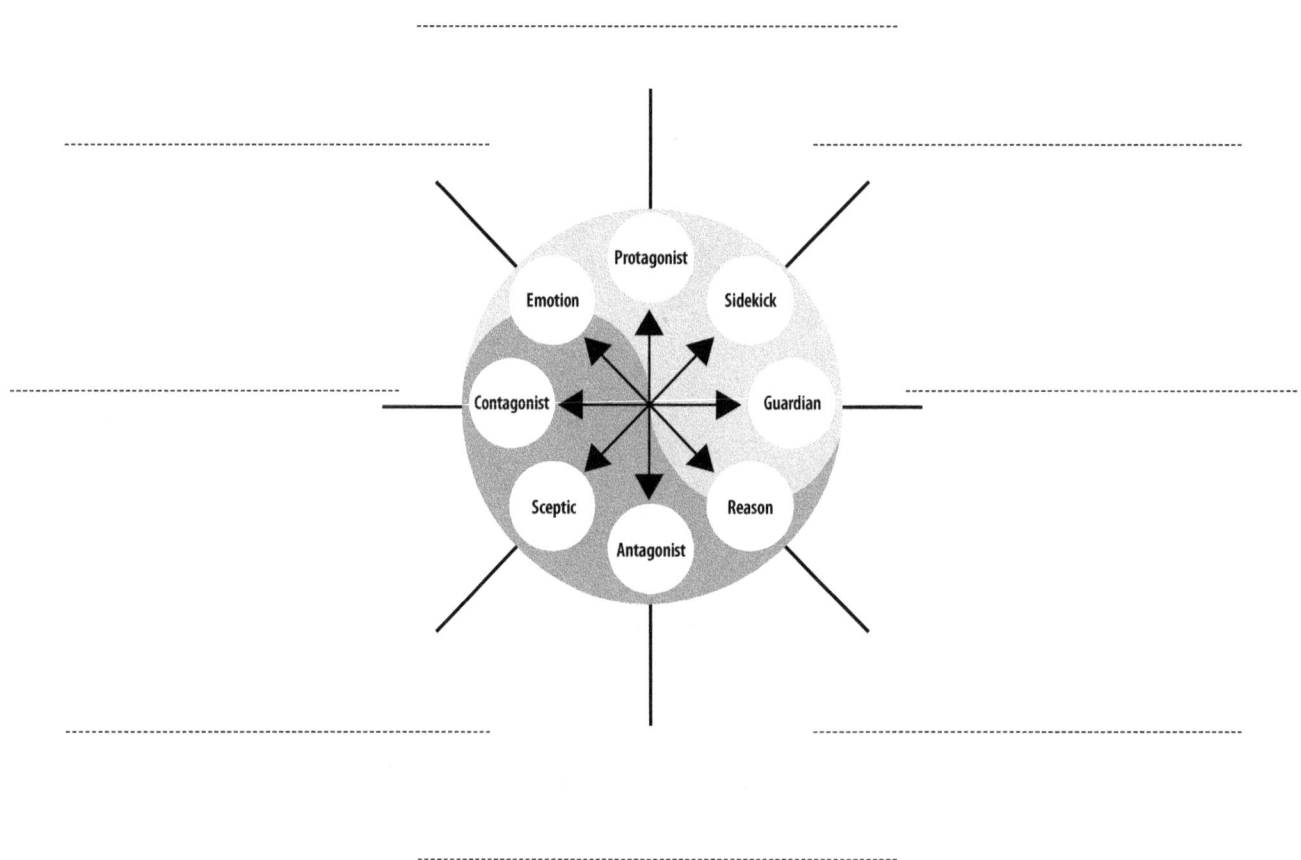

NOTE: It is not essential that your story has ALL archetypal roles filled.

Protagonist:

Name ....

Brief description ....

Goal (What do they want?) ....

Weakness (Hidden need) ....

Special talent ....

Conflicts with other characters ....

....

Antagonist:

Name ....

Brief description ....

Conflict with Protagonist ....

Source of dark power ....

Weakness ....

Conflicts with other characters ....

....

Guardian:

Name ....

Brief description ....

Relationship to Protagonist ....

Moral value (challenge to Protagonist) ....

Special powers, knowledge etc. ....

How does this character function to provide help to Protagonist? ....

....

Weakness and conflicts with other characters ....

....

Contagonist:

Name ....

Brief description ....

Relationship to Protagonist or Antagonist Weakness ....

Conflicts with other characters ....

Personal agenda (What they want) and trickery ....

Conflict with Guardian (over what moral value) ....

How does the character function to deflect the Protagonist from the goal? ....

....

Conflicts with other characters ....

Sidekick:

Name ....

Brief description ....

How they came to have a relationship with Protagonist ....

....

Particular characteristic the Protagonist values ....

....

Specific annoyance or aspect of conflict with Protagonist ....

....

Conflicts with other characters ....

Sceptic:

Name ....

Brief description ....

How they will test belief in the Protagonist and their goal ....

Type of conflict with Sidekick ....

Relationship to Antagonist ....

Conflicts with other characters ....

Reason:

Name ....

Brief description ....

How they will challenge the logic of the Protagonist's actions ....
....

Particular strength the Protagonist needs from this character ....
....

Conflicts with other characters ....

Emotion:

Name ....

Brief description ....

How they will influence Protagonist's sentimentality ....
....

Particular weakness the Protagonist has towards this character ....
....

Conflicts with other characters ....

Additional notes about your characters
....
....
....
....
....
....
....
....

Step 4: Create Your Story World

READINGS: THE PLAYGROUND (Story Craft I)

EXERCISE 4.1 Make a Map

This exercise was adapted from Holly Lisle's Settings Workshop in *Mugging the Muse*.

NOTE: For this exercise, you will need a sheet of A3 sized paper, a pencil or pen or coloured (fine point) markers but no erasers!

If you are doing this as a class group, have the group leader announce the instructions and work along. If you are doing this alone, without someone to announce the instructions, I suggest you read the instructions through to #10 below before you start drawing, just so you know what you are going to do. It's fun to do as a group. This exercise leads you through mapping your story world, but you can use exactly the same process to map regions, towns, locales, even houses. Do not attempt to make this a work of art, in fact, make it chaotic and busy. If you make a mark and didn't intend it to be there, do not rub it out — we have uses for it later.

Take 15-20 minutes to make the initial map.

Okay, let's begin. Using a separate sheet of A3 (large) paper and some marking instrument …

1. Place a dot on the page. Now place another dot in a different location. Put in a third dot.
2. Draw some upside-down V's in a line. These are your mountain range so they should necessarily not be in a straight line, they can have some gaps to allow for passes. Name the range. You can have more than one. You can vary the height, or double up sections.
3. Draw some snaky lines from the mountain range outward in a couple of directions. These are waterways — rivers or creeks, give them names.
4. Draw some broken (- - - - - - -) lines separating at least two of the dots from each other. These are borders between states, councils, countries, tribes, groups … Name the areas on either side of each border.
5. You might care to sketch in a lake or a desert or fields.
6. If you give yourself a shoreline (another long, wavy, wobbly line) stick some islands offshore. Don't forget jetties, docks and reefs where ships come to grief.

7. Use cloud shapes to doodle in a forest, oblique lines for woodlands and clumps for grassland.

8. Name the dots you've already drawn – they're your major centres, make them bigger. You might want to include some roads and railways and other important infrastructure.

9. Draw a few more dots in interesting places, and name them too — towns, settlements, mines, hideaways …

10. Find a couple of out-of-the-way places in your drawing and plonk in a couple of squares. These are dead places such as ruins from previous civilizations. Call them whatever you want.

Did you make mistakes?

11. Find the places where you wanted to erase — perhaps you drew a line someplace where it didn't belong, or you changed your mind later, like putting a mountain in the ocean. That's okay. That strange thing you added was designed by engineers. Really it was. It's an aqueduct, or a canal, or a tunnel or a missile silo … You have a road that goes nowhere? That's cool – somebody made it, and it used to go somewhere, and now all you have to do is figure out who made it, and where it used to go, and why it doesn't go there any more. Things do have to end sometimes, and sometimes that end is nowhere. It might have something scary there.

12. You have a ruin-box in what accidentally became a lake, or an ocean? No problem. Once upon a time that ruin was above ground. Or maybe it wasn't, and once upon a time there was a civilization that lived under the water.

This part of the exercise should take only 15-20 minutes.

Now put the art supplies away and answer the questions on the following eight pages. You can also notate your map, but if you do notate your map, make sure you transfer the notes to prose writing about your setting. You may also come up with other additions to your map as you write, keep working backwards and forwards, building the story world. Work quickly, writing ideas down as they come to you. This is about generating ideas, not about good grammar so do not spend time correcting mistakes or making sure it is neat (although make it neat enough to be read!).

Spend about five minutes on each question.

1. Why have people put in borders? A border always implies that conditions, people, philosophies, governments, or something else is different on each side. What are they protecting? From whom?

2. How are the people on different sides of borders different from each other? Religion, government, race, size, species ... go into detail, taking time working out what these differences are, and put some effort into figuring out why they were important enough to necessitate the creation of that border. Which side is your Protagonist's home side, which is your Antagonist's?

3. What goes up and down the rivers? (People, contraband, products, boats, other things ...) How does it get there? Who takes it? Are there dams and what are they used for?

4. What lives in the mountains? (Animals, people, big scary things, hermits, all of the above …) Describe the mountain life, how those living there survive, any tensions between high living folk and those of the lowlands.

5. How does the climate and weather endanger the lives of the people who live in the different parts of your world? Along with weather think about stuff like tornadoes, droughts, hurricanes, snowstorms, avalanches, tsunami, sandstorms and so on — you can include things like areas where you'll have earthquakes and volcanoes. Don't be afraid to be generous in heaping out troubles. You'll find plenty of use for them.

6. What else endangers the people here? Plagues, barbarians, illnesses, invaders, people from the other side of the world, monsters from the oceans or beneath the earth ...

7. Do a quick timeline in hundred-year increments, for maybe two thousand years. Write down one really big thing that happened in each of those hundred-year periods. It can be geological, political, religious, magical, whatever. But it needs to be big.

	-2,300 years
	-2,200 years
	-2,100 years
	-2,000 years
	-1,900 years
	-1,800 years
	-1,700 years
	-1,600 years
	-1,500 years
	-1,400 years
	-1,300 years
	-1,200 years
	-1,100 years
	-1,000 years
	-900 years
	-800 years
	-700 years
	-600 years
	-500 years
	-400 years
	-300 years
	-200 years
	-100 years
	Now

8. Write whatever else you can think of right now. Keep moving back and forth, from your map to your notes. Add stuff to the map as it occurs to you. Add stuff to the notes until something inside your brain goes "ding" and lets you know that you have a story world that you're genuinely excited about.

When you've finished, stick your map drawing into your notebook.

EXERCISE 4.2 Investigate Details

This exercise is to help you develop observation skills. *Spend 10-15 minutes on this exercise.*

1. Walk to a location outdoors and note down a list of things you see, smell and hear. Take particular note of the surroundings and note the details of the natural environment (the sky, trees, ground, weather, atmosphere, light, evidence of animals …) the man-made environment (buildings, gardens, domestic animals …) and the technological environment (power lines, solar panels, roads, cars …)

2. Move to another location and do the same.

3. Move indoors and do the same.

Be specific when you list what you see, hear and smell: describe these things in as much detail as you can, taking care to avoid the use of adjectives that generalise your descriptions (words such as 'big' and 'small' are of little value). Work quickly, simply jotting down your observations; touch surfaces and describe the feeling — if something is smooth, in what way is it smooth? Consider how tasteful a particular object might appear to you and how it fits within the environment. The important thing here is to use all five senses in your descriptions of what you are observing and be specific (using nouns and verbs) about the details.

Now return to your desk and write a short narrative of one of your characters coming into contact with that environment for the very first time. This is a stranger's response to the setting. Try to use as many of the details you observed as you can, weaving them into the character's experience. *(10 – 15 minutes)*

Now, taking exactly the same details, write a short narrative of another of your characters leaving that environment for the last time — they will never return to it. Again, try to use as many of the details you observed as you can, weaving them into the character's experience. *(10 – 15 minutes)*

EXERCISE 4.3 Your Story's World

Using your experience from the two previous exercises, write a short description of the location where your story takes place. Consider that your story might move from a location of the 'world of the everyday' through some sort of 'portal' to a 'mythological woods' (such as how Harry Potter moves from the muggle world to Hogwarts). Focus on the special world of the story, providing details such as those you discovered in the observation exercise above. Describe what you see, hear and smell; how it feels, what taste is present. Remember to be specific.

(300-500 words)

Step 5: Conflict

READINGS: CONFLICT AND THE FORCES OF OPPOSITION (Story Craft I)

EXERCISE 5.1 Discuss the Following

What does your Protagonist want?

Why do they (he or she) not have it at the beginning of the story? (In other words what is preventing them from having the thing they most want right now? Is it an internal attitude, or an external obstacle?)

If your story has a McGuffin, what is it? — the object that everyone wants (e.g. buried treasure), or wants to keep away from (e.g. disease).

What does your Antagonist want?

The answers to the above questions will help you determine what central conflict you are trying to resolve by the events of your story. Write a simple short statement:

The central (core) conflict of my story is

EXERCISE 5.2 Hidden and Contradictory Attributes

Make a list of character attributes of your Protagonist that you will *keep hidden* until the last possible moment: (Note: Don't make this too exhaustive ... 2 or 3 for each will be more than ample.) Remember these are the kinds of things that will only be revealed under great pressure from the oppositions of other characters. Then make a second list of three or four character attributes that may be contradictions (in other words, the character may act one way, but think another).

HIDDEN ATTRIBUTES

Physical	Sociological	Psychological

CONTRADICTIONS

Physical	Sociological	Psychological

Write about how such hidden attributes and contradictions might be revealed...

EXERCISE 5.3 Conflict and the Story World

What does the central conflict of the story tell you about where the story takes place and when?

Divide the story world into visual opposites based on how the characters oppose one another — (look at the oppositions of the main character archetypes ... what part of the story world 'belongs' to the Antagonist, what part 'belongs' to the Guardian and so on ... Use your story world map as a guide and find oppositions in the things you see, such as mountains/plains, under/above the sea, cities/villages, hi-tech/lo-tech, upstairs/downstairs ... and write about these oppositions in the space below.)

Examine the three elements of your story world (natural, man-made, technology) in terms of how they impact on the central conflict of the story. What is the nature of the portal between the world of the everyday and the mythological woods? What obstacles are placed in front of it? What prevents immediate return?

....

....

....

....

What obstacles from *Physical Space, Social Institutions* and *Influential Individuals* of society impact upon the Protagonist's progress towards his goal?

Physical Spaces

....

....

Social Institutions

....

....

Influential Individuals

....

....

How Does Time Affect the Stages of the Protagonist's Progress?

....

....

....

....

Step 6: Develop Your Plot and Step Sheet

READINGS: PLOT AND STRUCTURE (Story Craft I)

EXERCISE 6.1 Genre

What Genre are you writing in?

Explain two key concepts of this particular genre?

What books/stories have you recently read in this genre?

EXERCISE 6.2 The Plot: Devising the Master Plan

Which of the seven basic plots best suits your story?

Give a brief explanation of why

In your story, what happens to your Protagonist in each of the stages of the story ... (you should explore the conflicts, rising tension and character growth in each stage of your story by following your Protagonist through the story).

In the status quo

In the inciting incident

In the progressive complications

In the crisis

In the climax

In the resolution

EXERCISE 6.2 Your Step Sheet: Breaking down the Master Plan

Taking each of the stages you have outlined in your plot, map out the scenes of the story. Provide enough detail to know who is in the scene, what happens to them, how the action of the scene rises and falls. While there is no fixed number of steps, you should step out the sequences of your story so that you can follow it through logically from the beginning to the end. I recommend you use 12 - 14 steps in your sequence for a short story. Be prepared to work backwards and forwards, and leave plenty of working space to add in extras that you may discover.

Status Quo

Inciting Incident

Complication #1

Complication #2

Complication #3

Crisis

Climax

Resolution

Step 7: Moving Ahead

Pitching your Story

At this stage, you should be ready to begin writing your story. You should know your story well enough to be able to tell it in a three-minute pitch.

A 'pitch' is a verbal telling of the story so that a 'publisher' would be inclined to buy it. You need to stand in front of your group and pitch them your story. This is an important part of the process. Writing and delivering your pitch is not the writing of your story, it does not contain all the juicy action, snappy dialogue and gory battles, but it does tell the audience what they can expect when they read your story. It produces the pleasure they seek because it will lay out the structure in a way that helps them feel the suspense. More importantly it will test your own knowledge of your story.

The pitch will do a number of things:

- It will help you know your story
- It will help you develop confidence in your creative work
- It will highlight any 'plot holes' or weaknesses where the story doesn't hang together
- It will ensure the story ending works
- It will help you start in the right place.

Getting Prepared

1. Review the definition of story in Story Craft I. Does your story tell of a change that takes place? Does it involve a worthy human character? (In other words is the character worth spending time with?) Does the story set out a series of episodes that tell of what the character does in order to get what they want? Do the episodes lead naturally from one to the other? (This should be the details of your step sheet.) Does the ending provide an experience of pleasure? (In other words, does the Hero get what they want? Does the Villain get their just desserts?)

2. Do you have a premise? Is there a point about the human condition that is important to you that your story sets out to argue? Can you say how a dramatic character goes through a dramatic struggle to reach a dramatic conclusion … in a simple, single sentence?

3. What is your snapshot statement? *This story is about* ... Have you got a title? (*Most* important!)

4. Who are your principal characters (Protagonist, Antagonist)? Do you know them well? Do you know the other characters involved? Do you know how they are connected to each other? Are they sufficiently different from each other? Do the differences between them serve the conflicts of the story?

5. Where and when does your story take place? Do you have a clear idea of the world of your story, its key features, how the characters fit into that world, how they move between the World of the Everyday and the Mythological Woods? Does the world of the story serve your premise naturally?

6. Do you have a clear understanding of the central or core conflict of your story? Is there a McGuffin? Have you created and placed sufficient obstacles in the path of the Protagonist towards their goal? Does your cast of characters contain sufficient conflict between them to carry the story through the middle?

7. Do you know what genre you are writing in? Have you considered any specific requirements of that genre decision? (Science fiction must have science; Fantasy must have magic; Horror must have supernatural; Romance must have attraction ...) Have you figured out the plot type of your story? Have you mapped out the six steps of the plot Master Plan? Have you broken that master plan down into a step sheet? Do the scenes in your step sheet contain sufficient detail for you to know how you will write each one? Do the scenes lead logically from one to the next? Do you have a satisfactory ending?

Writing Your Pitch

Your pitch should take about three minutes to present, telling of the Hero's journey though the story from start to finish.

Put your premise at the top, followed by your story snapshot statement.

Then your title. (Note: this is the most important word or phrase in your story. It is the first impression anyone gets of what is to come. Spend time on it.)

Then in 200-300 words narrate the events of the Hero from the beginning to the end. Try to cover some small details of who the Hero is, what they set out to do, where and when the story takes place, who or what their opposition is, what obstacles they must overcome to draw closer to their goal, what setbacks they encounter and how they finally accomplish their goal. This is a summary version, it should not contain any dialogue, it is simply a 'telling' of the highlights of the narrative.

Presenting your Pitch

Introduce yourself — give your name as author, the title of your story, the premise and snapshot statement, and then tell the story.

If you can do it without reading all the better, but if you have to read it, do so slowly. Try to seek eye contact with your audience as you go in order to gauge reactions — if none have nodded off, then you can assume you're on the right track. When you reach the end of your pitch, thank your audience and ask if they have any questions or comments.

Listen carefully to the questions and comments, that's where you learn of any potential 'plot holes'.

Onward: Writing Your Story

By this stage you should know your story so well, you should be able to sit and write it fairly quickly. Before you begin your writing, review all of your notes, your pitch exercise, and any questions or feedback that arose from that.

Try to write something on your story every day — 15-20 minutes every day is far better than 2 hours every week. In your writing practice, spend a few minutes reading and correcting what you last wrote before moving on to write new material. This has the benefit of keeping the memory of your writing fresh, and helps you with your editing process later.

First Draft

Try to write the first draft of your story as quickly as possible. However, even though you are writing quickly, you should still try to write accurately — check your spelling, use correct punctuation, paragraph and sentence structures as you go. It is far more tedious and difficult to fix simple grammatical errors later.

In your first draft, follow your step sheet religiously. Write each scene you have described as it unfolds, and try not to get bogged down on parts where you may not know enough — leave notes to yourself to come back to and move on. Sometimes it helps to write an ending early in the writing process and then go back to fill in earlier sections. This helps maintain focus on where you want the story to go.

Once you have completed the first draft, read it thoroughly without spending time making corrections. After reading, think about how well you think it answers the premise you started with. Look for sections where you may have got sidetracked from the step sheet — do these deviations add to the story or detract from it? If you have left sections of the story empty because you did not know enough, do the research that will help you write those parts.

Redrafting

You should be prepared to write three drafts. Your first is a draft to get your step sheet into its logical story and the scenes developed. You need to spend a little more time on your second draft refining your characters' interactions and the details of your story world, and completing scenes that may have been left unfinished in the first draft.

In the second draft, consider choosing your beginning a few paragraphs in from the one you used in the first — there's a good chance that your character will be better revealed and the action more interesting. Try to improve your language. This doesn't mean get a thesaurus out over every word, it's more about reducing unnecessary repetitions, using better sentence structures, varying sentence structures, finding harder sounding words for action sequences, softer sounding words for gentler sequences making sure the dialogue is in conflict. In other words, put a little more concentration into the writing and less into the story itself — be poetic.

When you've finished your second draft read your work carefully. Careful reading is looking closely at every word, every sentence, every paragraph. Make sure they are correctly spelled, the tenses are correct, and you've chosen the right words for what you want to say. Make corrections to these things.

Read your work out loud. This important step forces you to slow down and read everything on the page. If you find yourself skipping sections, it's a sure sign that something is wrong. Try to find out what it is. Make sure the story works. The ending should have a natural connection with the beginning. There should be rising tension through the middle — if there's not, you can be pretty certain that conflict is lacking.

Final Draft

A third draft (no this is not editing) should only be undertaken after you've spent time on the above steps. By this stage you will know your story well, and be aware of some of its weaknesses.

In your third draft, you should be considering things like the order of events, making sure that flashbacks and story questions are in the right places to propel the story forward, the growth of the main character — do they become whole? — is there poetry in the ending; does the beginning start with a promise?

In this draft you are refining the story structure more than the language (which you concentrated on in the second draft). When you've finished the third draft, you should be ready for a reader.